My First Day at School

Rebecca Hunter

Photography by Chris Fairclough

Evans

First Times
My First Day at School
My First School Play
My New Sister
My First Visit to Hospital
My New Dad
Moving House
My First Pet
My First Visit to London

Published by Evans Brothers Ltd
2A Portman Mansions
Chiltern Street
London W1M 1LE
England

First published in 2000

Hunter, Rebecca
My first day at school, - (First Times)
1. First day of school - Juvenile literature
I. Title
372

ISBN 0 237 52016 8

Acknowledgements
Planning and production by Discovery Books
Editor: Rebecca Hunter
Photographer: Chris Fairclough
Designer: Ian Winton
Consultant: Trevor Jellis M.A., M.Phil., A.F.B.Ps., Psychol. is a Chartered Psychologist who has spent thirty years working with individuals, schools, companies and major corporate institutions in the management of stress. He deals with individuals who are suffering from stress both in their family and in the workplace.

The publishers would like to thank Roshaurn Lee, Dionne Waite, Mrs Gardner and the staff and pupils of Harborne Infants School, Birmingham for their help in the preparation of this book.

Contents

Today is my first day at school.

Today is my first day at infant school. Mum takes me to school. My little sister comes too.

Mrs Gardner is my new teacher.

My new teacher is Mrs Gardner.
She shows me where the toilets
are and
where to
hang my
coat. I say
goodbye
to Mum.

We go to assembly.

My teacher takes me to assembly. All the children sit down in a big room. The headteacher tells us a story from a book.

This is my new classroom.

This is my new classroom. The room is full of other children. I hope they like me.

Mrs Gardner gives us some paper.

I sit down with the children.
Mrs Gardner gives us all some
paper and crayons.
She asks me what I
am going to draw.

10

I draw a giraffe.

I draw my favourite animal. It is a giraffe. Mrs Gardner pins our pictures on the wall.

We go out to play.

At half past ten we
go out to play in
the playground.
We play games and run around.
This is my new friend Harprit.

Emily shows me the computer.

After playtime a girl called Emily shows me how to draw on the computer. I have never used a computer before. It is fun.

It is time for lunch.

It is lunchtime. I follow the other children to the dining room. We get in the queue. I am worried I won't like the food.

I sit down with my lunch.

When I am given my lunch I find a place to sit down. A teacher helps me cut it up.

Mrs Gardner reads us a story.

After lunch we sit down to listen to Mrs Gardner. She reads us a story from a big book.

We look at the books in pairs.

Now we have our own books.

We look at the books in pairs.

Harprit can read some of the words. I look at the pictures.

I build a tower.

Next we have free play. We can choose what to do. I am building a tower out of bricks.

It's time to go home.

It is time to go home.
Mum is waiting
outside for me.

I tell her about
the computer
and playing
with Harprit. I
think I'm going
to like school.

Index